ANTI-SEMITISM
Hatred on the Rise

Craig E. Blohm

San Diego, CA

About the Author
Craig E. Blohm has written numerous books and magazine articles for young readers. He and his wife, Desiree, reside in Tinley Park, Illinois.

© 2025 ReferencePoint Press, Inc.
Printed in the United States

For more information, contact:
ReferencePoint Press, Inc.
PO Box 27779
San Diego, CA 92198
www.ReferencePointPress.com

ALL RIGHTS RESERVED.
No part of this work covered by the copyright hereon may be reproduced or used in any form or by any means—graphic, electronic, or mechanical, including photocopying, recording, taping, web distribution, or information storage retrieval systems—without the written permission of the publisher.

Picture Credits:

Cover: Steve Edreff/Shutterstock.com

- 4: Shutterstock.com
- 5: Shutterstock.com
- 8: Shay Horse/ZUMA Press/Newscom
- 11: Pictures from History/Bridgeman Images
- 14: PVDE/Bridgeman Images
- 17: Shawshots/Alamy Stock Photo
- 21: Jim Ruymen/UPI Photo Service/Newscom
- 25: Brendt A Petersen/Shutterstock.com
- 27: Associated Press
- 30: Pictorial Press Ltd/Alamy Stock Photo
- 33: rituais em viagem/Shutterstock.com
- 36: Maury Asseng
- 41: Monkey Business Images/Shutterstock.com
- 45: Associated Press
- 46: ZUMA Press Inc/Alamy Stock Photo
- 49: neftali/Shutterstock.com
- 50: Gorodenkoff/Shutterstock.com
- 54: lev radin/Shutterstock.com

LIBRARY OF CONGRESS CATALOGING-IN-PUBLICATION DATA

Names: Blohm, Craig E., 1948- author.
Title: Anti-semitism : hatred on the rise / by Craig E. Blohm.
Other titles: Hatred on the rise
Description: San Diego, CA : ReferencePoint Press, Inc., 2025. | Includes bibliographical references and index.
Identifiers: LCCN 2023050459 (print) | LCCN 2023050460 (ebook) | ISBN 9781678207847 (library binding) | ISBN 9781678207854 (ebook)
Subjects: LCSH: Antisemitism--History--Juvenile literature. | Jews--Persecutions--Juvenile literature.
Classification: LCC DS145 .B614 2025 (print) | LCC DS145 (ebook) | DDC 305.892/4--dc23/eng/20231120
LC record available at https://lccn.loc.gov/2023050459
LC ebook record available at https://lccn.loc.gov/2023050460

CONTENTS

Important Events in the History of Anti-Semitism   4

Introduction   6
The Oldest Hatred Enters the Twenty-First Century

Chapter One   10
The Long History of Anti-Semitism

Chapter Two   20
Violence Against Jews

Chapter Three   29
Anti-Semitic Intimidation

Chapter Four   39
Fueling the Fire of Anti-Semitism

Chapter Five   48
Responding to Anti-Semitism

Source Notes	57
Organizations and Websites	60
For Further Research	61
Index	62

IMPORTANT EVENTS IN THE HISTORY OF ANTI-SEMITISM

63 BCE
Romans conquer Jerusalem and begin rule over Judea (Israel).

1933
Adolf Hitler becomes chancellor of Germany.

1880
Mass immigration of Jews to the United States begins.

70
Romans destroy the Second Jewish Temple in Jerusalem.

1543
Martin Luther writes anti-Semitic treatise *On the Jews and Their Lies*.

100 BCE / 100 CE   1500   1900

33 CE
Jesus of Nazareth is crucified by the Romans.

1903
The Protocols of the Elders of Zion is published.

1924
The Immigration Act of 1924 drastically reduces Jewish immigration.

1938
The *Kristallnacht* riot destroys Jewish businesses and synagogues.

1939
Germany invades Poland and begins World War II.

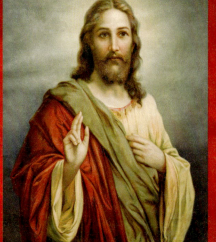

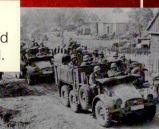

1942
The first mass gassing begins at the Belzec death camp in Poland.

2022
White supremacists organize a National Day of Hate against Jews.

2019
A gunman kills one person and wounds three at the Chabad of Poway synagogue in San Diego County.

1945
World War II ends, and the horror of the Holocaust is exposed for the world to see.

2017
The Unite the Right rally in Charlottesville, Virginia, leaves one dead.

1950   2000   2020

1958
The Hebrew Benevolent Congregation Temple, a synagogue in Atlanta, is bombed.

2018
Eleven Jews are murdered at the Tree of Life synagogue in Pittsburgh.

1941
The Nazi "final solution" declares that all Jews should be exterminated.

2023
President Joe Biden announces the US National Strategy to Counter Antisemitism; war between Israel and Hamas leads to a dramatic spike in anti-Semitic acts in the United States and other countries.

INTRODUCTION

The Oldest Hatred Enters the Twenty-First Century

On January 15, 2022, worship services at Congregation Beth Israel in Colleyville, a suburb of Fort Worth, Texas, were interrupted by an armed gunman who took four people hostage, beginning what would become an eleven-hour standoff. In November of that year, Jewish residents of North Bethesda, Maryland, discovered that vandals had painted hateful graffiti, including swastikas and figures being hanged, on private and public property. Three months later in Los Angeles, two Jewish men were shot and wounded outside a synagogue by a man who had a history of sending anti-Semitic text messages. Despite occurring in widely separate locations, these three incidents had one thing in common: they were all attributed by investigators to anti-Semitism, the discrimination against or hostility toward people of the Jewish faith.

A History of Intolerance

For thousands of years Jews have been subjected to prejudice, harassment, and violent attacks. As they began to spread throughout the known world from their Middle Eastern homeland in the sixth century BCE, anti-Semitic discrimination followed them. Enslaved and then exiled by the Egyptians, the Jews were tolerated in the Roman Empire until 70 CE, when the Romans put down a Jewish revolt and destroyed their temple in Jerusalem.

In America anti-Semitism existed even before the Revolutionary War. Peter Stuyvesant, director general of the New Netherland colony, strove to keep Jews out of New Amsterdam (later to become New York City), and anti-Semitic rhetoric was common in colonial newspapers. During 1880 to 1920, millions of Jews immigrated to America, fleeing violence in Europe. But they could not escape anti-Semitism, which grew as the Jewish population expanded. By the 1930s immigration laws limited the number of Jews who could gain refuge in the United States from harassment and persecution.

World War II saw horrific persecution of Jews by the Nazis, who murdered some 6 million Jews in the Holocaust. In America after the war, anti-Semitism declined as part of a revival that saw people of all faiths placing renewed emphasis on religion. Jews found acceptance and prosperity in society. This trend continued through the civil rights era of the 1950s and 1960s, the Vietnam War in the 1960s and 1970s, and the often-turbulent decades that followed. But anti-Semitism had not completely disappeared, and eventually open hatred of Jews and other minorities reared its ugly head once more.

Anti-Semitism Today

The twenty-first century is witnessing a disturbing increase in the expression of hatred toward Jews. Brian Levin, director of the Center for the Study of Hate and Extremism at California State University, San Bernardino, notes, "We're in a new era for anti-semitism. We're now seeing Jews becoming a default target."[1] This new era includes mass attacks on Jewish congregations, harassment in person and online, and hate groups that espouse conspiracy theories about Jews plotting to take over America.

The Anti-Defamation League, an organization dedicated to fighting anti-Semitism

> "We're in a new era for antisemitism. We're now seeing Jews becoming a default target."[1]
> —Brian Levin, director of the Center for the Study of Hate and Extremism

White supremacists march at the Unite the Right rally in Charlottesville, Virginia, in August 2017. Emboldened by a changing political climate, hate groups organize rallies and disseminate anti-Semitic material.

and other forms of prejudice, reports that in 2022 incidents against Jews in the United States increased by 36 percent over the previous year, the largest rise in the organization's forty years of tracking incidents. Other nations with large Jewish populations have also experienced an upsurge in anti-Semitism, motivated by the increase of far-right politics and by COVID-19 conspiracy theories that falsely blame Jews for creating and spreading the virus. No Jews are immune to anti-Semitism, from Jewish children bullied by their schoolmates to elderly Jews suffering from unprovoked assaults.

The increase in attacks on Jews is explained in part by the popularity of social media, which can be used by anti-Semitic individuals and groups to spread lies and inflammatory information to a wide, often uncritical, audience. White supremacists and other right-wing hate groups are emboldened by the changing political climate in the United States, organizing rallies and disseminating anti-Semitic material. Another motive for anti-Jewish activities lies in the Middle East territory of Palestine, once controlled by Arab and Jewish peoples. Both have long considered this land their home and sanctuary. But the founding of the nation of Israel in 1948 left Palestinians without a permanent home. Jews have since come under intense condemnation and hostility from the Arab community. US support for Israel since its beginning has prompted recurring incidents of anti-Semitic violence in America.

Because anti-Semitism has been a threat to Jews for thousands of years, it is often called "the oldest hatred." Yet it remains all too prevalent in the twenty-first century and is growing more virulent in the United States every day. Eradicating the scourge of anti-Semitism would ultimately mean not only freedom for Jews but a better world for all.

CHAPTER ONE

The Long History of Anti-Semitism

The violence began shortly before midnight on November 9, 1938. In towns and cities across Germany, the sounds of breaking glass and the crackling of fire as buildings went up in flames marked the beginning of an all-night violent attack against German Jews. Nazis roamed through the streets, smashing windows of Jewish shops and setting fire to Jewish homes, businesses, and synagogues. Eleven-year-old Albert Friedlander was a young Jew living in Berlin. He later described the destruction he and his father saw as they wandered through their devastated neighborhood. "There was a lot of glass on the streets. We lived in the West End, surrounded by shops, many of them Jewish. This was late at night and it was dark; but we had no trouble in picking out the Jewish shops. They had been looted, the windows had been smashed, and there were ashes, rubble and debris outside some of the shops."[2]

The violence inflicted on the Jews that November came to be known as *Kristallnacht*, or "Night of Broken Glass." The Nazis destroyed 267 synagogues and vandalized and looted more than seven thousand Jewish businesses. At least ninety-one Jews were killed, and thirty thousand Jewish men were arrested and sent to concentration camps. Kristallnacht was the first step leading to the Holocaust and the extermination of 6 million Jews. But it was not the first time Jews had been targeted for their faith. Judaism has a history of persecution that goes back more than two thousand years.

The Early Roots of Anti-Semitism

Most of the societies of the ancient world were polytheistic, meaning that people believed in numerous gods. The ancient Egyptians, for example, worshipped some fifteen hundred gods, including Isis, Ra, Osiris, and Horus. The Babylonians revered Marduk as the patron god who protected their nation, but they worshipped many other deities as well. Jewish belief, however, ran counter to the idea of a pantheon of gods.

As recounted in the book of Exodus, Moses, a prophet of the Israelites (as Jews were called in ancient times) received the Ten Commandments from God on Mount Sinai. In the first of these commandments, God states, "You shall have no other gods besides Me."[3] The Israelites were to worship only the one true God, ignoring the gods revered by other cultures. Called monotheism, this belief set them apart from the rest of the ancient Middle East. In the sixth century BCE, the Babylonians conquered the Jewish land and sent thousands of Jews into exile for not worshipping the Babylonian gods.

A synagogue in Frankfurt, Germany, burns after being set ablaze by anti-Semitic rioters. On November 9, 1938, Nazis across Germany vandalized thousands of Jewish businesses and destroyed 267 synagogues. The violence inflicted on Jews that night became known as Kristallnacht, or "Night of Broken Glass."

When Rome occupied their homeland in the first century BCE, the Jews learned to adapt to Roman customs while still maintaining faith in their God. But around 30 CE a radical itinerant preacher named Jesus was executed by the Roman authorities, who were pressured to do so by the Jewish religious elite. "His blood be on us and on our children,"[4] the Jews were said to have exclaimed. This pronouncement led to the belief that Jews of all generations bore responsibility for the death of Jesus, whom many believed to be a divine personage. It was one of the root causes of modern anti-Semitism.

Anti-Semitism Grows

During the first millennium CE, hostility grew against the Jews, who became an oppressed minority within the expanding sphere of Christianity. The Christian preacher Paul wrote that the Jews "killed both the Lord Jesus and the prophets."[5] During the First Crusade, a Christian campaign that began in 1096 CE to recapture the Holy Land from Muslim rule, some five thousand Jews were massacred by zealous crusaders bent on destroying all enemies of Christianity. As the Christian faith spread through western Europe, it brought with it an ancient, false idea of "blood libel," in which Jews supposedly kidnapped and killed Christian children to use their blood in Jewish rituals. Jews were also prohibited from owning land and working in certain occupations. At a thirteenth-century council meeting, the Catholic Church prohibited Jews from holding public office and mandated that they wear distinctive clothing that identified them as Jews.

In the sixteenth century, German priest and theologian Martin Luther published his Ninety-Five Theses, a treatise that led to the beginning of the Protestant Reformation. As a young monk, Luther had exhibited kindness toward Jews, but this tolerant attitude changed in his later years. In 1543 he authored *On the Jews and Their Lies*, in which he wrote, "Beware of the Jews . . . you can see how God's wrath has consigned them to the Devil, who has robbed them not only of a proper understanding of the Scriptures, but also of common human reason, modesty and sense. . . . Thus, when you see a real Jew you may with a good conscience cross yourself, and boldly say, 'There goes the Devil incarnate.'"[6]

> "When you see a real Jew you may with a good conscience cross yourself, and boldly say, 'There goes the Devil incarnate.'"[6]
> —Theologian Martin Luther

Luther also advocated burning Jewish schools and synagogues, confiscating Jewish literature, and silencing rabbis under threat of death. This inflammatory rhetoric has led some scholars to view Luther's stance as a foreshadowing of the ruthless anti-Semitism of Nazi Germany. It also led to another form of prejudice against the Jewish people. By the nineteenth century a new aspect of anti-Semitism arose, based not on the Jews' religion but rather the idea that they constitute a distinct and separate race. This racial anti-Semitism centered on physical stereotypes. For instance, Jews were portrayed in books and newspaper cartoons as having large noses and beady eyes. It also centered on social stereotypes. Many Jews held jobs in finance or ran successful shops or other businesses. This was used against them as they were often described as unethical, dishonest, and lazy.

No Jews Allowed

Excluding Jews from various organizations and activities has long been a feature of anti-Semitism. After the Civil War, wealthy Americans sought membership in a new trend called the country club. In these clubs, the elite could gather for camaraderie and to enjoy sports while escaping the commotion of the cities. There was, however, one unwritten rule: Jews were forbidden to join.

No matter how wealthy a Jew was, country club membership was reserved for non-Jews only. Some Jews joined restricted clubs by changing their name to a less Jewish-sounding one; others established their own clubs. But country clubs were not the only places where Jews were unwelcome. Many real estate companies practiced "redlining," refusing to sell homes to Blacks and Jews.

Many colleges and universities created quotas to restrict the number of Jews they would enroll. In the 1920s and 1930s, Harvard established strict quotas for Jews because it feared that the presence of Jewish students would discourage Christian applicants. In the 1950s Stanford University limited recruiting students from high schools that were predominantly Jewish.

Times and the laws have changed. Redlining is now illegal, universities can no longer discriminate through quotas, and most country clubs now welcome Jews.

Anti-Semitism in America

In the late nineteenth century, increasing prejudice and violence led many Jews to search for a safer homeland. For many of the millions of people who immigrated to the United States, their first glimpse of the Statue of Liberty in New York Harbor made a lasting impression. Seventeen years after the statue's dedication in 1886, a bronze plaque was added, on which a poem bore the words: "Give me your tired, your poor, your huddled masses yearning to breathe free."[7] Written by Jewish American poet Emma Lazarus, these words welcomed millions of Jews to American shores during the great migration of the late nineteenth and early twentieth centuries.

Between 1880 and 1920, more than 2 million Jews immigrated to the United States from Russia and other eastern European countries. For many of those immigrants, their first glimpse of the Statue of Liberty made a lasting impression.

Lazarus was inspired to write the poem, entitled "The New Colossus," by the suffering of Jews during a period of crushing poverty and brutal pogroms in Russia. From 1880 to 1920 more than 2 million Jews immigrated to the United States from Russia and other eastern European countries. These immigrants brought with them what few possessions they could carry. They also carried the long-held stigma of simply being Jewish.

Anti-Semitism in the United States intensified as more Jewish immigrants arrived. Many Americans viewed these newcomers with suspicion and hostility. The presumption that Jews were "Christ killers" remained strong among some Christians in the United States, where Christianity was the dominant religion. The majority of Jewish immigrants settled in large eastern cities such as New York. There they built new lives as they found work or established businesses and created vibrant social organizations—all of which helped them build close cultural ties with other Jews and participate in the spiritual fellowship of the synagogue. But anti-Semitism knew no geographical bounds, as author and historian Leonard Dinnerstein wrote: "Traversing the United States in the 1890s one found abundant evidence of open hostility to Jews in both rural and urban areas. In northeastern Iowa and northwestern Illinois Jews were not welcome in the civil and general affairs of the communities while intermarried Jews were scorned by their own coreligionists and barely tolerated by Christians."[8]

> "Traversing the United States in the 1890s one found abundant evidence of open hostility to Jews in both rural and urban areas."[8]
>
> —Historian Leonard Dinnerstein

In 1924, new laws set limits on the number of immigrants allowed to enter the United States from countries around the world. Like others who had hoped to immigrate, Jews from Europe were caught up in this change. By this time the US Jewish population stood at about 3.5 million. But they were a people apart, struggling to fit into a new world that, like the old world they left behind, embraced deep-seated prejudices toward them.

The Holocaust

In 1933 Adolf Hitler, the leader of the Nazi Party, became chancellor of Germany. The German people, and their nation's army, had been demoralized by defeat in World War I. When he assumed office, Hitler immediately began rebuilding the army and rallying his people. He also devised a plan to rid Europe of Jews. Hitler's hatred of Jews was well known. In his manifesto *Mein Kampf* ("My Struggle"), published in 1925, Hitler wrote, "[The Jew] stops at nothing, and in his vileness he becomes so gigantic that no one need be surprised if among our people the personification of the devil as the symbol of all evil assumes the living shape of the Jew."[9] On September 1, 1939, the German army invaded Poland, igniting World War II.

> "[The Jew] stops at nothing, and in his vileness he becomes so gigantic that no one need be surprised if among our people the personification of the devil as the symbol of all evil assumes the living shape of the Jew."[9]
>
> —German chancellor Adolf Hitler

As German troops marched through eastern Europe, anti-Semitic laws were passed, and Jews were socially isolated, their businesses boycotted. Jews were required to wear a yellow Star of David patch on their clothing, a symbol of their segregation and humiliation. In 1941 Nazi general Reinhard Heydrich was given orders to make preparations "necessary for carrying out the desired final solution of the Jewish question."[10] By January 1942 the "final solution" was decided: all of Europe's Jews were to be exterminated.

Dachau, the first Nazi concentration camp, opened in 1933 to house Marxist and Communist political prisoners. It became the model for future camps designed to hold and execute Jews. In 1941 Chelmno, the first camp specifically constructed to murder Jews, began operation. Jews were herded into gas chambers on the pretext of showering. Once sealed, the chambers were filled with poison gas, which killed the victims in a matter of minutes. Estimates of Jewish victims killed at Chelmno range from 150,000 to 200,000. By the end of the war, around 6 million Jews had been sent to their deaths in thousands of camps located within Germany and its occupied territories.

The bodies of Jews murdered by Nazis are stacked, awaiting cremation at the Buchenwald death camp in Germany in 1945. By the end of World War II, around 6 million Jews had been killed in concentration camps located within Germany and its occupied territories.

The names of other infamous Nazi death camps have remained forever etched into the memories of the relatives and descendants of their victims. These include Auschwitz, Treblinka, Sobibor, Buchenwald, and Majdanek. These camps represent the worst anti-Semitic horror suffered by the Jewish people.

Anti-Semitism in the Twenty-First Century

After World War II the United States entered a period of peace and prosperity. The economy boomed, with factories that formerly made tanks and ships now manufacturing cars, furniture, and household appliances. The strong economy of the 1950s was balanced by the growing uncertainties of the Cold War, which pitted the United States against the Soviet Union in a struggle for economic and military superiority. This atmosphere of hope and anxiety created a spiritual revival as church attendance rose and religion gained a renewed significance for the uncertain modern era. Jews were a part of this revival, building new synagogues and settling into the mainstream of American life. Social restrictions on

Henry Ford: Auto Magnate and Anti-Semite

Henry Ford will always be remembered for making automobiles affordable for the masses and for creating the mobile society we now enjoy. But there was a darker side to Ford that encompassed his unsavory attitude toward Jews.

By 1919 Ford was acknowledged as the foremost automotive manufacturer in America. He was also a zealous anti-Semite who blamed Jews for all of society's ills. He bought a failing newspaper called the *Dearborn Independent* and for seven years used its pages to publish articles advancing his anti-Semitic theories. Backlash against Ford's extremism eventually caused the *Independent* to cease publication, but its influence had already reached a wider audience.

When Adolf Hitler wrote *Mein Kampf*, he included quotes from Ford's newspaper articles. In 1931 the Nazi leader told a reporter, "I regard Henry Ford as my inspiration." In 1938 Hitler bestowed on Ford a medal called the Grand Cross of the Order of the German Eagle. Although Henry Ford's contributions to American industry will always be admired, the man behind them remains an unfortunate example of the power of prejudice.

Quoted in Bill McGraw, "Henry Ford and the Jews, the Story Dearborn Didn't Want Told," Bridge Michigan, February 4, 2019. www.bridgemi.com.

Jews, such as rules banning them from membership in exclusive clubs, were eased, as were quotas on Jewish college applicants. Anti-Semitism seemed to be waning. Historian Dinnerstein optimistically stated in 1994 that anti-Semitism in America "has declined in potency and will continue to do so for the foreseeable future."[11]

One phenomenon that most people could not foresee was the rise of the internet in the twentieth century. The internet has become a ubiquitous feature of modern life. It is also an indispensable medium for extremist groups to broadcast their ideologies and recruit new followers into their world of hate. "Social media platforms, unwittingly or not, have facilitated [antisemitism], and are, therefore, implicated in the violence that emanates from it,"[12] writes Cassie Miller of the Southern Poverty Law Center, a nonprofit organization that fights all forms of hate through legal action.

The changing political climate in America is also a factor in a renewed rise of anti-Semitism. In his inaugural address on January 20, 2017, President Donald Trump stated, "From this day forward, it's going to be only America first. America first."[13] It is unknown whether Trump was aware that "America first" had been used in the early 1940s as an anti-Semitic figure of speech by those who felt Jews were trying to force the United States to enter World War II. Trump's use of the slogan, which had also been employed by the Ku Klux Klan, a White supremacist group formed shortly after the Civil War, was condemned by the Anti-Defamation League for its anti-Semitic connotations. Jewish historian Deborah Dash Moore noted that radically conservative groups, such as the Proud Boys and Oath Keepers, would commend Trump's words: "Those groups in fact do know their history, and they do recognize where the term comes from."[14]

The increase in anti-Semitism in twenty-first-century America is hard to miss. Nazi flags that promote White supremacy fly at rallies. Attacks on Jews have escalated at an alarming rate. Anti-Semitic literature, graffiti, and other forms of harassment are cropping up in neighborhoods all across the country. Tropes about Jews possessing too much wealth and power or being an inferior race have resurfaced. The world's oldest hatred is once more on the rise.

CHAPTER TWO

Violence Against Jews

The twenty-first century has witnessed a surge of violence against Jews in the United States. The Anti-Defamation League reported a 26 percent rise in violent anti-Semitic incidents in 2022 over the previous year. Five states—California, Florida, New Jersey, New York, and Texas—accounted for more than half of all anti-Semitic incidents in the United States. New Jersey has the third-largest percentage of US Jews, at nearly 6 percent of the state's population. With a recent increase in anti-Semitic incidents in the state, the Federal Bureau of Investigation (FBI) warned synagogues to increase their security measures and be vigilant. Rabbi David Levy, director of the American Jewish Committee's New Jersey office, called the FBI's notice "a reflection of rising antisemitism in our country and how that antisemitism can morph into violence."[15]

Violent Encounters

Violent acts against Jews in the United States are not a new phenomenon. In the late 1950s Atlanta, Georgia, was the scene of an explosion that shattered the Hebrew Benevolent Congregation Temple, the city's oldest synagogue. The temple suffered massive damage when fifty sticks of dynamite exploded in the early morning hours of October 12, 1958. The bomb blew a huge hole in the temple's exterior brick facade, shattered stained glass windows, and damaged numerous offices and Hebrew school classrooms. While the sanctuary received little damage, the schoolrooms were unusable until a rebuilding finance campaign was organized. Fortunately, the building was unoccupied at the time of the blast and no one was injured.

Five members of the White supremacist National States Rights Party (NSRP) were arrested in connection with the bombing. Their avowed reason for targeting the historic synagogue was that Jews—especially the temple's rabbi, Jacob M. Rothschild—were behind the emerging civil rights movement that advocated equality for Blacks. Although brought to trial in December 1958, none of the bombers were found guilty.

The bombing of the temple was not an isolated incident. Local investigators and the FBI determined that the incident was part of a campaign of terror directed at Jews across the southern United States in 1957 and 1958. It was the culmination of a series of bombings and attempted bombings of Jewish synagogues, schools, and community centers in Alabama, Mississippi, Florida, and other southern states by the NSRP and other groups.

Incidents of anti-Semitic violence continued in the following decades. A synagogue in Gadsden, Alabama, was the target of an attempted firebomb attack during a service in March 1960. The bomb fell short of its target, exploding against the synagogue's

A mother comforts her daughter following an attack by a gunman on the North Valley Jewish Community Center in Granada Hills, California, in 1999.

outer wall. As two men ran from the building to investigate, the bomber—a sixteen-year-old boy—shot and wounded them with a rifle. During the civil rights era, Jews generally supported Blacks in their struggle for freedom, a stance that opened Jews to anti-Semitic threats. Notices stating "Jews Not Allowed" often accompanied "Whites Only" signs at public facilities. In 1964 three civil rights workers, two of them Jewish, were slain in Neshoba County, Mississippi, by members of the Ku Klux Klan. On August 10, 1999, a gunman armed with a semiautomatic weapon fired seventy rounds in the North Valley Jewish Community Center in Granada Hills, California. Three boys, one of them six years old, and two adults were wounded.

Most anti-Semitic assaults have resulted in injury rather than death, but they still strike fear in the Jewish community. Assailants usually resort to punching, kicking, and otherwise physically striking their victims rather than using deadly weapons such as knives or guns. But it was only a matter of time before anti-Semitic violence escalated to a horrific event causing mass casualties.

Rampage at the Tree of Life

On the cool and drizzly morning of Saturday, October 17, 2018, the Tree of Life synagogue in Pittsburgh, Pennsylvania, was hosting Shabbat, or Sabbath-day, services. Tree of Life is located in Squirrel Hill, a Pittsburgh neighborhood with a large Jewish population. Members of three congregations—New Light, Dor Hadash, and the synagogue's own members—shared the facility and were gathered in various areas of the building that morning.

Waiting outside was a forty-six-year-old man named Robert Bowers, who had written numerous anti-Semitic posts on social media such as "Jews are the children of Satan." Bowers was obsessed with fear of minorities taking over, in his words, "my people," by which he meant the White race. On this Saturday morning, he posted a final, ominous message: "I can't sit by and watch my people get slaughtered. Screw your optics, I'm going in."[16] At 9:50 a.m. Bowers entered the synagogue armed with an

The Lynching of Leo Frank

On April 27, 1913, the body of thirteen-year-old Mary Phagan was discovered in the basement of an Atlanta factory where she worked. In one of the most controversial murder cases in US history, the man convicted of the crime became the only known Jew to be lynched in America.

Leo Frank, the thirty-one-year-old factory superintendent, had paid Phagan her wages the day before her body was found. Frank was arrested and charged with the crime, and at his trial he was found guilty of murder. Frank was sentenced to death. Public opinion turned against him; Jewish businesses were boycotted, and many Jews fled the city. In June 1915, after a reexamination of the evidence, Frank's sentence was commuted to life in prison. But an anti-Jewish mob had a different idea of justice. On August 17, 1915, a group called the Knights of Mary Phagan kidnapped Frank from his cell and hanged him from a tree.

Historians believe that Frank was innocent of Phagan's death and that a janitor at the factory was likely the murderer. But his death reverberated across America. It played a part in the founding of the Anti-Defamation League, but it also encouraged a revival of the Ku Klux Klan.

---

assault-style rifle and three handguns. Worshippers scattered in terror as gunfire echoed through the halls of the synagogue, but for many there was no escape.

A 911 call summoned police a few minutes after the gunman began his rampage. When officers arrived, they were pinned down by Bowers's gunfire. Soon the shooter ran to the third floor of the synagogue and tried to hide, but police eventually located him. Wounded, Bowers was arrested and taken to a hospital, still declaring that he wanted all Jews to die. The rampage at Tree of Life was over, but the outcome was devastating. Eleven worshippers died in the massacre and six people were wounded, including four police officers. The victims ranged in age from fifty-four to ninety-seven. Among those killed were Bernice and Sylvan Simon, who had been married at Tree of Life sixty-two years earlier, and Cecil and David Rosenthal, disabled brothers who regularly volunteered at the synagogue.

Bowers recovered from his injuries and was tried on thirty counts of murder and hate crimes. On August 1, 2023, a unanimous jury sentenced him to death. As for the Tree of Life, the synagogue has been closed since the tragedy in 2018. But in

2023 plans were under way to reopen the building with a new addition containing a center for combating anti-Semitism and a memorial to the eleven victims of the worst act of anti-Semitic terror in US history.

Targeting Jews

Experts study incidents such as the mass murders at Tree of Life to try to understand what makes someone like Robert Bowers kill innocent people simply because of their religion. Influenced by the rhetoric of anti-Semitic propaganda from social media and far-right hate groups, synagogue shooters hold Jews responsible for maliciously influencing every facet of life, from instigating wars and manipulating the global economy to controlling the world's governments and even affecting the climate for their own benefit.

Jews have been accused of having a vast secret agenda to achieve what conspiracy theorists say is their objective of world domination. "The core of modern antisemitism is primarily based on a fear of perceived Jewish power and strength," notes a report by the nonprofit Counter Extremism Project. Conspiracy theorists, the report goes on to say, believe that "the Jew is the enemy that needs to be defended against."[17] Viewing Jews as the "enemy" provokes many anti-Semitic individuals and groups to turn to violence.

> "The core of modern antisemitism is primarily based on a fear of perceived Jewish power and strength."[17]
>
> —Counter Extremism Project

Some people may dislike or fear things that seem strange to them or that they do not understand. To many, Jews can fall into those categories. In the United States, with a Jewish population of some 7.6 million (out of a total of 332 million), it is likely that the majority of Americans personally know few, if any, Jews. Unfamiliarity with and lack of understanding of a group of people can breed an irrational hatred. Writer and social commentator Micah Halpern distinguishes what he calls Jew-hatred from anti-Semitism. "Jew-hatred is a visceral hate," he explains. "It is emotional, it is not at all rational. . . . Antisemitism is based on principles. It is wrong—but it

Eleven people were killed and six were injured in an attack on the Tree of Life synagogue in Pittsburgh, Pennsylvania, on October 17, 2018.

is not visceral. It is based on a set of ideas. Today's Jew-hatred is filled more and more with anger and vitriol."[18]

It is that anger and vitriol that have led to tragedies such as the Tree of Life massacre. Others would soon follow.

Jews Under Fire

Poway is a quiet, middle-class city of about fifty thousand residents in San Diego County in California. Serving the city's Jewish community are several synagogues, including the Orthodox Chabad of Poway. Just six months after the Tree of Life massacre, an anti-Semitic gunman unleashed a murderous rampage at the Chabad synagogue.

On Saturday, April 27, 2019, the last day of the Jewish Passover holiday was being celebrated by about fifty members of the Chabad of Poway. At 11:23 a.m. nineteen-year-old John Timothy Earnest, wearing tactical armor and armed with an AR-15-style rifle, entered the synagogue and began shooting. Within a few minutes one woman, sixty-year-old Lori Gilbert-Kaye, was dead and three people, including the synagogue's rabbi, were

Terror at the Supermarket

Anti-Semitic violence has become a global scourge. The Hyper Cacher kosher grocery store in Paris, France, was the scene of a brutal attack in January 2015 by a radical Islamist named Amédy Coulibaly. Coulibaly stormed the store carrying several semiautomatic weapons, immediately shooting one man at the store's entrance. He then began taking more than a dozen hostages, including a child and an infant, threatening them with death.

During the four-hour siege, Coulibaly was in contact with several French journalists, admitting that he had specifically targeted the Jewish market. Zarie Sibony, a cashier at the store who survived the attack, later quoted Coulibaly as telling the hostages, "You Jews, you like life too much when what's important is death. I'm here to die. You are Jews and French, the two things I hate the most." Coulibaly killed three more hostages before being shot to death by French special forces troops.

France has the largest Jewish population in western Europe, estimated at some 450,000. But as anti-Semitic incidents increase, many French Jews now wonder about their safety.

Quoted in Kim Willsher, "Cashier Tells of Four-Hour Ordeal in Paris Supermarket Siege," *The Guardian* (Manchester, UK), September 23, 2020. www.theguardian.com.

---

wounded. As Earnest fired, he was heard shouting anti-Semitic slurs. Quickly exiting the building, possibly because his rifle had jammed, Earnest fled in his vehicle. As he sped away, he called 911, boasting to the dispatcher, "I'm defending my nation against the Jewish people, who are trying to destroy all white people."[19]

Earnest ultimately surrendered to law enforcement and was placed on trial. In 2021 he was sentenced to two life sentences, one by a California court for the murder of Gilbert-Kaye and the other in a federal verdict that found him guilty of hate crimes.

In 2022 Lakewood, New Jersey, a township of nearly 140,000 residents near the Atlantic shore, had a deadly encounter with anti-Semitism. Two-thirds of Lakewood's population is made up of Orthodox Jews. With numerous synagogues and the Beth Medrash Govoha—a yeshiva, or college for Orthodox studies—this peaceful town has become a center for the Orthodox Jewish faith in America. On April 8, 2022, that peace was shattered by a ten-hour anti-Semitic crime spree.

> "I'm defending my nation against the Jewish people, who are trying to destroy all white people."[19]
>
> —Poway synagogue shooter John Timothy Earnest

It all began around 1:00 p.m. when twenty-seven-year-old Dion Marsh carjacked a Toyota Camry, assaulting the driver in the process. At 6:00 p.m. Marsh deliberately drove into and critically injured a man. Soon after this attack, Marsh exited the car and stabbed another man in the chest, and at 8:20 p.m. he rammed the car into yet another person. All of Marsh's victims were Orthodox Jews, easily identifiable by their black hats and long black coats. Marsh was arrested around midnight and taken into custody. When asked the reason for his crime spree, Marsh told police that "it had to be done," and that Orthodox Jews "are the real devils."[20]

Protecting Against Violence

In the aftermath of the violent attacks on Jews at Squirrel Hill and Poway, Jewish leaders nationwide began searching for ways to protect their congregations. Some of these measures were already in place by September 2019, when Rabbi Joshua M. Davidson and his congregation came together to celebrate Rosh Hashanah, the Jewish New Year, at Temple Emanu-El in New York City. On this usually joyous occasion, the atmosphere surrounding the historic synagogue was different. "As we entered," Davidson remarked, "none of us could help notice how our threshold is different this year

Many synagogues now rely on local police or private security personnel to keep watch and deter attacks by extremists.

> "The boulders on the sidewalk, the scanners, the security guards—who ever would have imagined that here on Fifth Avenue these would be necessary to keep us safe? We have become a fortress."[21]
>
> —Temple Emanu-El rabbi Joshua M. Davidson

than last. The boulders on the sidewalk, the scanners, the security guards—who ever would have imagined that here on Fifth Avenue these would be necessary to keep us safe? We have become a fortress."[21]

Like Temple Emanu-El, many synagogues hire security guards to protect worshippers while they attend services. These guards can range from off-duty or retired law enforcement officers to private security personnel to armed members of the congregation who have police or military backgrounds. Plainclothes officers can provide discreet protection with minimal disruption, while uniformed guards at synagogue entrances are a visual deterrent to violent acts.

Courses in security methods help many synagogues create a safer environment. Many nonprofit organizations offer seminars and training on what to do if a congregation finds itself in an active-shooter situation. Other security measures include installing security cameras, keeping doors locked, installing metal detectors, and reinforcing windows. Protection does not come cheap, however. A synagogue in Long Island, New York, spent about $150,000 on security measures. The US Department of Homeland Security offers grants that can help with the financial burden of security installations for smaller congregations.

Houses of worship have fundamental vulnerabilities that may be difficult to set aside. For example, they traditionally keep their doors open to anyone who is in need, but this openness can lead to danger. In 2022 a man looking for shelter was welcomed into Congregation Beth Israel synagogue near Dallas, Texas. Before long, he was holding four men at gunpoint in an eleven-hour standoff. Safety training courses taken by the rabbi helped the hostages escape the dangerous situation unharmed.

Turning a house of worship into an armed fortress goes against everything that religious faith stands for. But as anti-Semitism turns more violent, congregations must respond to that new reality.

CHAPTER THREE

Anti-Semitic Intimidation

On May 3, 2023, Adam Miller had just left a school board meeting in Naples, Florida. Miller, the senior rabbi at Temple Shalom of Naples, was at the meeting to speak about the impact of rising intolerance on Jewish and other minority students. As Miller walked toward his car, two men approached him and began shouting anti-Semitic insults at him, including, "Your prophet is not real, and Judaism is not a real religion. You're on the path to sin."[22] The rabbi was shaken by the encounter but remained calm. "Their tone was very hateful and angry" he says, "and they would not stop following me."[23] Miller endured the incident without escalating the confrontation.

Such incidents of anti-Semitic harassment are, unfortunately, not rare. The Anti-Defamation League (ADL) defines anti-Semitic harassment as verbal or written slurs, stereotypes, or conspiracy theories directed at Jewish people. According to the ADL, in 2022 there were 2,298 incidents of anti-Semitic harassment, an increase of 29 percent over 2021. Given our uncertain political world, such incidents are likely to continue. "History is flashing warnings to the world," says CNN's senior political reporter Stephen Collinson. "Outbursts of antisemitism have often been harbingers of societies in deep trouble and omens that extremism and violence are imminent. . . . History does not end. It merely slumbers, then repeats itself."[24]

Anti-Semitic Symbolism

If, as the old saying goes, a picture is worth a thousand words, then symbols that denigrate Jews can speak volumes about hatred and marginalization. The ADL studies the use of symbolism in anti-Semitism and has created a comprehensive online database of hate symbols.

The swastika, one of the most commonly used anti-Semitic symbols, has become a familiar sight at far-right rallies and on anti-Semitic literature and websites. An ancient cultural and religious emblem, the swastika is a cross having arms of equal length bent at 90-degree angles. Originally a symbol of good luck, examples of the swastika have been found at archaeological sites dating back ten thousand years or more.

In the twentieth century Hitler's Nazis turned the swastika into a mark of hatred for Jews, adorning flags, buildings, and military uniforms with the *Hakenkreuz*, or hooked cross, as they called it. In the aftermath of the Holocaust, the swastika has become the

Hitler's Nazis turned the swastika into a mark of hatred for Jews. In the aftermath of the Holocaust, the swastika has become the ultimate anti-Semitic symbol.

ultimate anti-Semitic symbol. Its use is now banned in Germany, France, Israel, Russia, and numerous other nations. In the United States the First Amendment right of freedom of speech allows the display of swastikas without government interference.

Along with the swastika, other symbols are used by anti-Semites to harass Jews. The Civil War Confederate battle flag has been adopted by far-right groups. Its design consists of two diagonal blue stripes bearing thirteen white stars on a red field. Often incorrectly referred to as the official flag of the Confederacy, the battle flag is today a pervasive symbol of hostility toward minority groups. The swastika and the Confederate battle flag are the two most prominent emblems displayed at White supremacist rallies. The cross, an enduring symbol of Christianity, is also sometimes used in the logos of supremacist groups, most notably the Ku Klux Klan. Another symbol, which is becoming common online, is the so-called echo. Placing three sets of parentheses around a person's name, as in (((John Doe))), indicates to those who are familiar with the symbolism that the person is Jewish and thus a target for harassment.

> "We must secure the existence of our people and a future for white children."[25]
>
> —White supremacist slogan

Symbols can also support anti-Semitic views using specific numbers or hand gestures. The number *88*, for example, is often found in White supremacist literature and on social media sites. The numeral *8* represents the eighth letter of the alphabet—*H*—and thus *88* stands for *HH*, or "Heil Hitler" in the far-right lexicon. This number is often paired with the number *14*, which stands for a fourteen-word phrase that promotes White supremacy: "We must secure the existence of our people and a future for white children."[25]

A common hand gesture, formed by creating a circle with the thumb and index finger and extending the other fingers, has long been a symbol meaning "okay." White supremacists have turned this innocent sign of approval into a hate symbol: the extended fingers forming a *W*, and the circle and palm forming the letter *P*, which together stand for "White power."

Shoelaces as a Political Statement

Most people give little thought to the humble laces that keep their shoes securely on their feet. The color of shoelaces can be a fashion statement, but it can also signify affiliation with certain groups or viewpoints. The Anti-Defamation League, which studies all forms of anti-Semitic communication, points out that red laces can denote a neo-Nazi, or someone who has spilled blood for the cause. White laces signify White supremacy, while blue laces are sometimes an indication of killing a police officer. Black laces are generally neutral and make no statement. Purple can stand for gay pride, while yellow denotes antiracism.

The manner in which shoes are laced can also have a particular meaning. While shoes are generally laced in a crisscross pattern, using "ladder lacing" gives a distinctive look. Originated by military paratroopers, ladder lacing arranges the laces straight across, giving the appearance of a ladder, another way for supremacists to identify each other.

White supremacists do not have a monopoly on shoelace symbolism. On the *Jewish Journal* website, designer Jonathan Fong provides a tutorial describing how to tie a Star of David with one's laces.

Hateful Words

Symbols can be a visible way to communicate contempt for Jews, but words carry a weight that is especially hurtful. In May 2021 a group of some three hundred people in Boca Raton, Florida, held an outdoor rally in support of Israel. During the peaceful gathering, several men drove past the crowd in a white van whose sides were painted with numerous anti-Semitic slogans, including "Hitler Was Right," and "Holocaust Never Happened." Rabbi Efrem Goldberg, who recorded video of the incident, commented, "We rally for peace and this van filled with hate, call[ing] for genocide and threats kept circling. . . . Hard to believe in the heart of Boca Raton if didn't see it myself."[26]

> "We rally for peace and this van filled with hate, call[s] for genocide and threats kept circling. . . . Hard to believe in the heart of Boca Raton if didn't see it myself."[26]
>
> —Rabbi Efrem Goldberg

Hateful words, especially those invoking Hitler and the Holocaust, are often used to threaten and intimidate Jews. One phrase that appears often in White supremacist writings is the German *Arbeit Macht Frei*. Translated as "Work Sets You Free," it was the inscription emblazoned over the entrance to Auschwitz, a notorious Nazi death camp. During the Holocaust, more than 1 million

Jews were forcibly transported to the camp. Expecting to be put to work, most of them were instead put to death in the camp's gas chambers. For the remaining survivors and for the living descendants of those who perished at Auschwitz, these three words are a painful reminder of the evil that anti-Semitism can beget.

The far-right organization Goyim Defense League (GDL) is a White supremacist group that uses words to harass Jews. The members have adopted the Yiddish word for non-Jews (*goyim*) as their name. They are dedicated to producing anti-Jewish propaganda. In 2022 they carried out 370 incidents of propaganda distribution across 43 states. One of their tactics is hanging harassing signs or banners on highway overpasses. In Jacksonville and Daytona Beach, Florida, GDL members unfurled banners bearing anti-Semitic slogans over a busy expressway. The group is also known for its distribution of anti-Semitic flyers in residential areas and for creating pamphlets that claim Jews are the underlying cause of everything from COVID-19 to abortion and the policies of both the Trump and Biden administrations.

Perhaps the most hurtful insults are the personal ones aimed at Jewish individuals. Reprehensible anti-Semitic slurs such as *hebe*,

White supremacists often use the German phrase Arbeit Macht Frei, which translates as "Work Sets You Free." The inscription was emblazoned over the entrance to the notorious Nazi death camp, Auschwitz (shown).

jewboy, *hymie*, and *kike* are used to abuse and humiliate Jews. Determining the proper response to this harassment creates a dilemma. Retaliation to insults with further insults can cause a bad situation to become worse, possibly leading to physical violence. Not responding, however, may indicate an inclination to meekly suffer such abuse and thus add legitimacy to the harassment. As a result, many Jews have decided to avoid certain places and situations that could make them vulnerable to anti-Semitic harassment.

Harassment at School

While being persecuted for your religious beliefs is difficult enough for adults to cope with, Jewish children and teens also suffer being bullied and taunted at school. In 2022 a study of anti-Semitism in public and private middle and high schools was conducted by the Jewish Community Relations Bureau and American Jewish Committee in three urban areas of Kansas. The study found that 89 percent of Jewish students saw or experienced some form of anti-Semitism at school or online. This harassment often took the form of telling "Jew jokes," promoting Jewish stereotypes, denying that the Holocaust happened, and creating anti-Semitic graffiti. One student quoted in the survey commented, "A girl thought because she knew me she could make Jew jokes and Holocaust jokes and made me incredibly uncomfortable. . . . [A] friend also told me 'If I make a gas chamber joke you're just going to have to deal with it.'"[27] The study concluded that "unfortunately, we continue to see that Jewish students in our region are confronted by anti-Semitism on a disturbingly regular basis, in their schools and on social media."[28] At the college and university level, anti-Semitic harassment is, if anything, even more prevalent than in the lower grades.

On US college campuses students can exchange new ideas, explore broad avenues of thought, and examine the opinions of those who are of different races, ethnicities, and religions. Despite the campus atmosphere of freedom of thought and belief, anti-Semitism has gained a hold at many colleges and universities as Jewish students cope with harassment and discrimination. In 2022

Denying the Holocaust

One of the most insidious means of harassing Jews is promoting the idea that the Holocaust did not happen. The Holocaust is the twentieth century's most extreme example of the atrocities of anti-Semitism. To deny the systematic killing of 6 million Jews strikes at the very heart of Jewish identity. It suggests that their existence and their deaths have no meaning.

White supremacist groups such as the Goyim Defense League use Holocaust denial (also called Holocaust revisionism) as anti-Semitic harassment, claiming that the Holocaust was fabricated by Jews to gain sympathy and also for monetary gain. The term *Holohoax* is often used in anti-Semitic social media postings.

Among famous writings about Nazi atrocities is a diary kept by Anne Frank, a Jewish girl in Netherlands who spent over two years hiding from the Nazis before being discovered and ultimately perishing in a concentration camp. Deniers claim that her diary is a fraud, but researchers have thoroughly debunked this assertion. Frank's diary remains an authentic reminder that the Holocaust was all too real.

---

more than 130 US colleges and universities experienced incidents of anti-Semitism. Often, these are cases of vandalism, with swastikas inscribed on Jewish dormitories, as well as "Heil Hitler" and references to the Holocaust. Many Jewish students follow the tradition of hanging a mezuzah, a small piece of parchment inscribed with a prayer and enclosed in a decorative container, on the doorframe of their dorm room. Numerous cases of vandals desecrating or removing these symbols of Jewish heritage have been reported, including at prestigious institutions such as Stanford University, Ohio State University, and George Washington University.

College life is stressful enough without having to deal with anti-Semitic harassment. "Antisemitism can dramatically affect a student's college experience," says Elissa Buxbaum, the national director for college and university programs at the ADL. "It only takes one act of antisemitism against a college community to make all Jewish students at that campus feel unsafe or unwelcome."[29]

> "Antisemitism can dramatically affect a student's college experience. It only takes one act of antisemitism against a college community to make all Jewish students at that campus feel unsafe or unwelcome."[29]
>
> —Anti-Defamation League's Elissa Buxbaum

Vandalism and Desecration

Anti-Semitic harassment in the form of vandalizing Jewish property is on the rise in Jewish neighborhoods as well as on high school and college campuses. This vandalism includes actions such as spray-painting swastikas on buildings, painting derogatory language such as "Death to Jews" and "Hitler was right" in public spaces, and making other references to the Holocaust. According to the ADL, anti-Semitic vandalism in 2022 increased by 51 percent over the previous year.

A Decade of Anti-Semitic Incidents in the United States

Anti-Semitic incidents have been increasing in the United States over the last decade. Data gathered by the Anti-Defamation League (ADL), an organization that fights anti-Semitism and other forms of prejudice, shows the largest increase between 2021 and 2022. During that period, anti-Semitic hate crimes grew by 36 percent to a record high of 1,124. Data used for this graph only goes through May 2023. Since the October 7, 2023, Hamas attack on Israel, the ADL says, anti-Semitic incidents in the United States have risen by 388 percent.

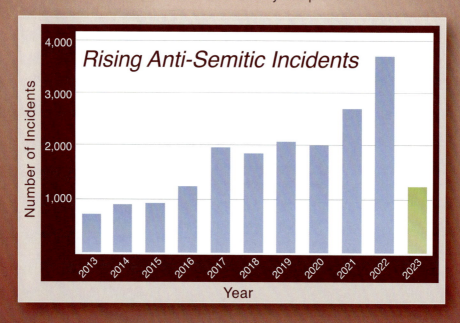

Source: Tori Morales Pinales, "How Reports of Hate Crimes in the US Were Already at Record Highs, in 4 Charts," CNN, October 29, 2023. www.cnn.com.

Vandalism targets more than just buildings. In 2017 about one hundred headstones were toppled in a Jewish cemetery in Philadelphia, and in 2022 thirty-nine Jewish headstones were vandalized with painted swastikas and other graffiti in the Congregation Am Echod Jewish Cemetery in Waukegan, Illinois. The destruction or defacing of Jewish religious items is also a problem. These incidents range from the historic destruction of Torah scrolls (handwritten parchment scrolls containing the first five books of the Hebrew Bible) by the Nazis during Kristallnacht to present-day vandalism of many such scrolls found in modern synagogues. On January 14, 2023, a woman broke into Temple Emanu El in Houston, Texas, and caused thousands of dollars' worth of damage to the temple and several religious items, including Torah scrolls kept there. A week later she returned to the temple, shouting and frightening children during a Shabbat service.

Online Harassment

Along with the increase in personal attacks on Jews, the problem of online harassment is also growing. For example, TikTok, with more than 1 billion users worldwide, saw a 912 percent increase in anti-Semitic content in 2020 and 2021. This content may be obvious, using text, images, or videos that are explicitly anti-Semitic. Or it can be subtle, such as words with hidden or double meanings, various symbols or numbers, or "dog whistle" phrases that secretly denote hatred of Jews to those who are familiar with the hidden connotation. An example of a dog whistle is the word *globalist*, which is widely used to surreptitiously indicate Jews, referencing their supposed conspiracy to dominate the world.

The COVID-19 pandemic forced a drastic reduction of in-person contact as people avoided assembling in groups. Soon social media began replacing such face-to-face gatherings with online worship services, school classes, and business meetings. Zoom, a videoconferencing platform, became a popular way to conduct business meetings and distance education without fear of spreading the virus. Before long, however, some people began to use the platform for malicious purposes. In a method called "Zoombombing," hackers would break into online conversations, disrupting business, educational, religious, and other Zoom sessions with pornography and hate speech. Such speech often included anti-Semitic images and messages.

In 2020, at the height of the pandemic, a Zoom session was about to begin at a Conejo Valley Unified School District meeting in California when hackers attacked. Participants' computer screens were suddenly filled with images of swastikas, Nazi troops, and Adolf Hitler, as well as threats of violence against school board members. Other Zoombombing attacks have occurred across the United States. In Ohio a religion class at the B'nai Jeshurun synagogue was taken over by hackers, who played audio of violent sounds and chants of "Heil Hitler." At Yeshiva University in New York City, about 150 students watching the university president's Passover speech on Zoom were assailed with an anti-Semitic tirade that included Holocaust memes and death threats. Even a virtual Jewish funeral service in Cleveland, Ohio, was Zoombombed, with mourners being told that the deceased "deserved to die."[30]

Whether anti-Semitic hate is displayed on the internet, scrawled on synagogue walls, or shouted in verbal assaults, it is the malicious root of the enduring harassment that Jews find themselves struggling against every day.

CHAPTER FOUR

Fueling the Fire of Anti-Semitism

In February 2023 law enforcement agencies across the United States began preparing for the possibility of a new and violent wave of anti-Semitic hatred. Touted on social media as a National Day of Hate, the planned event was promoted by White supremacist groups, which warned that Jews would be targeted on Saturday, February 25, the Jewish Shabbat. Organizers used the social media app Telegram to tell followers to "make your voices heard loud and clear, that the one true enemy of the American people is the Jew."[31]

People were urged to participate in the event by displaying anti-Semitic banners, scattering leaflets, and defacing property with swastikas and other graffiti. They were also told to take photos or record video of their actions to spread the hate across the internet. Many police departments across the United States increased patrols in an effort to stem any potential violence and admonished Jews and Jewish organizations to be extra vigilant. Ultimately, no increase in anti-Semitic activity was reported on the so-called National Day of Hate. But the fact that such a threat could trigger a nationwide scare attests to the power of racial and religious hatred to travel far and wide.

Flyers of Hate

Although the National Day of Hate never materialized, the spread of anti-Semitic propaganda did not stop. On September 11, 2023, residents of the Del Cerro neighborhood of San Diego, California, awoke to a disturbing sight. Overnight, anti-Semitic flyers had been placed on car windshields in the community by persons unknown. The date of this incident is significant because the flyers reportedly contained anti-Semitic disinformation about the 9/11 terrorist attacks.

It was not the first time that this quiet community had been flooded with hate literature. In July of that year, residents of Del Cerro and other nearby communities with large Jewish populations similarly discovered anti-Semitic flyers placed on car windshields during the night. These flyers contained hate-filled falsehoods targeting Jews, including denial of the Holocaust and its 6 million Jewish victims. Some leaflets also attacked the LGBTQ community. The local communities involved had seen an increase in anti-Semitic harassment in the months between these incidents, and residents are now fearful of what may follow. While no one has been charged in connection with these acts, officials believe that the far-right group GDL may have been behind the distribution. But even if the culprits are caught, under current law the crime has no significant consequences. The San Diego City Council is seeking to increase the penalty for spreading such hate-speech literature.

The ADL says that this type of harassment is growing within several anti-Semitic groups and is becoming a nationwide problem. In Wellington, Florida, for example, some one hundred anti-Semitic flyers sealed in plastic bags were dropped on driveways and in yards. Among other lies, the leaflets blamed Jews for the COVID-19 pandemic. Similar pamphlet drops were made in Marietta, Georgia; Kirkland, Washington; Oklahoma City, Oklahoma; and other locales.

Distributing flyers or other printed material by hand is a simple though labor-intensive method for spreading hate. But with the advent of the internet, anti-Semitic literature can travel at the speed of light.

Social Media and Anti-Semitism

Technology is the latest weapon in the arsenal of anti-Semites who derive satisfaction from attacking the Jewish community. This is first and foremost achieved today by the widespread use of social media. Although the amount of online anti-Semitic content is only a small fraction of overall global social media posts, it is still a major problem, especially for impressionable youth. A report entitled *The State of Antisemitism in America 2022* by the American Jewish Committee reveals a startling statistic: "Eighty-five percent of Jews ages 18–29, compared to 64% of those age 30 or older, reported they experienced antisemitism online or on social media. Further, among those Jews who experienced antisemitism online, younger Jews (26%) were more likely than older cohorts (14%) to say these online incidents made them feel physically threatened."[32]

Popular social media platforms such as Facebook, TikTok, X (formerly known as Twitter), YouTube, and Instagram have all been used to propagate anti-Semitic misinformation. While these platforms make efforts to monitor and remove hate speech, it is difficult to completely eliminate such messages and tropes. Other platforms, touting free speech and no censorship, have become

The widespread use of mobile devices and social media has become the latest weapon in the arsenal of anti-Semites. A large majority of Jews report that they have seen anti-Semitic content on social media.

havens for far-right groups to spread their anti-Semitism. Telegram, a social network founded in 2013, experienced a surge of far-right followers when platforms such as Facebook and Twitter blocked their posts after the January 6, 2021, attack on the US Capitol. Since then, Telegram has expanded worldwide and in 2023 had more than 1 billion users. While most of these users are benign, some use Telegram to post anti-Semitic messages to a vast audience over numerous Telegram channels. And the messages can be disturbing. One prolific influencer frequently posts anti-Semitic tropes on Telegram. These run the gamut from Jewish world domination and anti-vaccine theories to claims that Jews were responsible for both world wars.

Other anti-Semitic extremists use social media to explain or justify their violent actions or to rant about their false ideas about Jews. The gunman in the 2019 Poway, California, synagogue shooting posted an anti-Semitic manifesto on the far-right platform 8chan (now renamed 8kun) shortly before beginning his attack. In the diatribe, he claimed, "Every Jew is responsible for the

War and Anti-Semitism

The October 2023 attack on Israel by the terrorist organization Hamas—and Israel's response to that attack—caused more than the death and destruction that has appeared daily in news reports around the world. It has also led to a huge increase in anti-Semitic incidents.

In the month after the October 7 strike, the Anti-Defamation League (ADL) recorded 832 instances of anti-Semitism in the United States. These incidents included harassment, vandalism, and physical assaults against Jews. This represents a 316 percent increase compared to the same month in the previous year. "When conflict arises in the Middle East," notes ADL national director Jonathan Greenblatt, "antisemitic incidents increase here in the U.S. and around the world."

The dramatic rise in anti-Semitic incidents in the United States has not escaped the notice of the American people. An ADL survey taken in October and November revealed that 71 percent of Americans now believe that anti-Semitism is a serious problem, up from 53 percent the previous year. In addition, 47 percent say they have become inspired to oppose anti-Semitism. Says Greenblatt: "This crisis of antisemitism demands a fierce response, and it's encouraging that nearly half of Americans feel personally motivated to address this challenge."

Quoted in "One Month Following Hamas Massacre, ADL Documents Dramatic Surge in Antisemitic Incidents in the U.S.," Anti-Defamation League, November 13, 2023. www.ADL.org.

meticulously planned genocide of the European race. . . . I only wish to inspire others and be a soldier that has the honor and privilege of defending his race in its greatest hour of need."[33]

Celebrity Influencers

If synagogue shooters like the Poway gunman seek to "inspire others," celebrities already have the means and the public platform to do just that. One morning in January 2023, students going to and from classes at the University of Alabama were confronted with the slogan "Ye is Right" scrawled in chalk on several campus sidewalks. The cryptic sentiment soon began to spread, often in the form of "Ye is right, change my mind" or paired with the words "America First."[34] Most people know that Ye is the megastar rap artist and fashion entrepreneur formerly known as Kanye West. But what was it that some people believed Ye was right about?

> "I'm going death con 3 On JEWISH PEOPLE."[35]
>
> —Rapper and entrepreneur Ye

The phrase became widespread as the result of a series of anti-Semitic comments Ye made beginning in October 2022. In a Twitter post, Ye stated, "I'm going death con 3 On JEWISH PEOPLE,"[35] misusing the military term *DEFCON 3*, which refers to a heightened threat level. The message was just one of Ye's many statements concerning Jews, repeating the standard tropes about Jews being greedy and bent on world domination, as well as expressing admiration for Adolf Hitler. This post, however, ended a lucrative partnership deal Ye had with the sportwear company Adidas.

While Ye's post was soon removed, its sentiment was quickly adopted by anti-Semitic groups. Members of the GDL displayed a banner reading "Kanye is right about the Jews" (a phrase that echoes the common anti-Semitic slogan "Hitler was right") over a freeway in Los Angeles while giving the Nazi salute to passing cars. Another White supremacist group organized an event called "Ye is right, change my mind" on several college campuses in January 2023. The events centered on anti-Semitic misinformation and encouraged students to participate in debates on Ye's beliefs.

Anti-Semitic Conspiracies

While celebrities may have an undue influence when disseminating misinformation about Jews, other sources can be just as persuasive to people who have fallen under the shadow of conspiracy theories. Based on intolerance and outright lies, anti-Semitic conspiracy theories have a long history of hostility toward Jews and are often offered by anti-Semites as a rationale for spreading their hate.

In 1903 a pamphlet called *The Protocols of the Elders of Zion* began circulating around Europe. Published in Russia, it presents itself as a true story that recounts the meetings of a group of powerful Jews who convene in Switzerland to plot Jewish world domination. Soon after its publication, the Russian secret police used the pamphlet to justify their violent pogroms against Jews. In Germany it provided a rationale for the growing anti-Jewish sentiment that Jews were responsible for Germany's loss in World War I. As Hitler's Nazi Party gained power in the 1930s, the pamphlet gave purpose to the ultimate Jewish tragedy, the Holocaust.

The Protocols of the Elders of Zion was exposed as a hoax in 1921. But it did not fade into obscurity. Throughout the years, the message of the pamphlet has been periodically revived by anti-Semitic groups as a rationale for their hatred of Jews. A modern version of this conspiracy theory is called the great replacement theory. According to this belief, people of White European ancestry are being replaced in their native countries by Black and Brown immigrants—and it is the Jews who are orchestrating this grand scheme. This idea has been adopted by White supremacist groups and individuals (like the Poway synagogue shooter), who use it as a rallying cry against Jews.

In August 2017 White supremacists held a rally called Unite the Right in Charlottesville, Virginia. The demonstrators made clear their anti-Semitic views, chanting "Jews will not replace us"[36] as they marched carrying Confederate and supremacist flags. One protester proclaimed, "Our country has been usurped by a foreign

> "Our country has been usurped by a foreign tribe, called the Jews. We're tired of it."[37]
>
> —Protester at Unite the Right rally

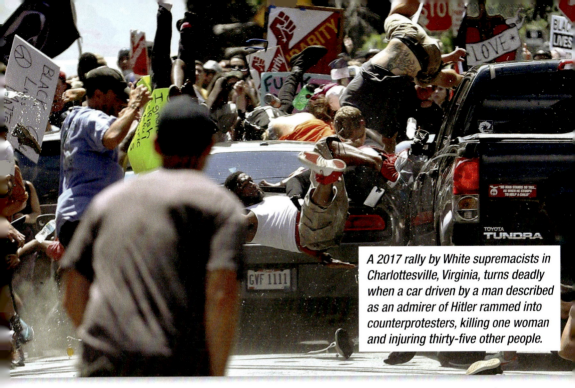

A 2017 rally by White supremacists in Charlottesville, Virginia, turns deadly when a car driven by a man described as an admirer of Hitler rammed into counterprotesters, killing one woman and injuring thirty-five other people.

tribe, called the Jews. We're tired of it."[37] Tensions flared when a group of counterprotesters arrived, and the rally soon took a tragic turn. Twenty-year-old James Alex Fields Jr. rammed his car at high speed into the counterprotesters, killing one young woman and injuring thirty-five other people. News reporters who investigated his background and interviewed people who knew him described Fields as an admirer of Hitler and a promoter of White supremacy.

Anti-Semitism and the Current Political Climate

Jewish history is the story of a people who for millennia wandered from place to place after being forcibly uprooted many times from their homes. Modern-day anti-Semitism and the horror of the Holocaust prompted a resurgence of Zionism, a late-nineteenth-century movement dedicated to creating a permanent nation for Jews in their ancient homeland, Palestine. In 1948 the nation of Israel was born, and with it the conflict between Jews and Arab Palestinians, who continue to fight to retain their own claim to the land.

The United States has supported Israel since its birth as a nation in 1948, prompting anti-Semitic rhetoric and actions by those who believe Palestinians are being robbed of their own land. This was most recently made evident by reaction to the war that began on October 7, 2023, with a deadly surprise attack on Israel by the militant Palestinian group Hamas. Incidents of anti-Semitism escalated as Palestinian supporters condemned Israel's massive and deadly counterattack. Pro-Palestinian rallies denouncing Israel spread across the United States, Europe, and the Middle East. At many of these rallies, protesters used well-known anti-Jewish slogans, blurring the line between political protest and personal attacks on Jews.

American colleges and universities were particularly affected by the backlash of anti-Israel demonstrations—and a rise in anti-Semitic language, harassment, and threatened violence. At Cooper Union college in New York City, student Taylor Roslyn Lent became alarmed by a pro-Palestinian demonstration. "I felt hated for my Jewish identity," she says. "There's definitely a big difference between a pro-Palestine–anti-Israel rally, and an anti-Jewish rally. And the more the day went on, the more it felt like an anti-Jewish rally."[38]

Conflict between Israel and Palestinians and a subsequent backlash against Israel has led to a rise in anti-Semitic language, harassment, and threatened violence on college campuses.

Algorithms and Anti-Semitism

Hidden within the phones, computers, and websites that people use every day are small pieces of computer code called algorithms. An algorithm is a sequence of steps used to complete a specific task. For example, Google employs an algorithm called PageRank that determines how high in a search result an item will be displayed. Algorithms make modern technology more user-friendly, but they also have a dark side.

Anti-Semitism on the internet can be spread by the use of algorithms that record a viewer's engagement, or how interested they are in a website. When someone visits a site containing information of Jewish interest, an algorithm notes the choice and can direct the user to other websites that may contain anti-Semitic content. Posting likes, dislikes, and even critical comments on anti-Semitic sites can trigger algorithms that spread such content even further.

But algorithms can also be used to fight online anti-Semitism. The Anti-Defamation League has developed an algorithm that can identify anti-Semitic online content and uses that information to work toward deleting offensive content.

Threats of violence filled the social media accounts of campus administrators and Jewish student organizations. On October 31, 2023, a junior at Cornell University in New York was arrested for allegedly making threats to Jewish students, saying he would "bring an assault rifle to campus and shoot all you."[39] Sometimes threats became reality. Earlier in October, several Jewish students were assaulted at Tulane University in New Orleans when a rally turned violent.

The rapid rise of campus unrest prompted the US Department of Education to issue a "Dear Colleague" letter on November 7, 2023. It reminded college and university administrators to adopt a "renewed urgency" in their efforts to provide a learning environment free from discrimination.[40]

A Troubling Development

Jews have made a tremendous impact in virtually all aspects of American society. Despite these contributions, they continue to experience prejudice and hatred from a vocal and hateful minority. Once largely relegated to the fringes of society, anti-Semitism has gained a place in the mainstream of American life—a troublesome development on numerous levels.

CHAPTER FIVE

Responding to Anti-Semitism

The United States was founded on the principle of freedom: of speech, of the printed word, and of religion. Perhaps no colony exemplified religious freedom more than Rhode Island, which is known for its dedication to liberty for all religions. In 1763 the colony's seaport town of Newport became the site of the first Jewish synagogue in the New World with the completion of the classically designed Touro Synagogue. In 1790 President George Washington wrote a letter to the congregation of Touro, reaffirming America's commitment to religious liberty by saying the government "gives to bigotry no sanction, to persecution no assistance."[41]

More than 230 years have passed since Washington wrote this letter. Despite his stirring words to the Jews of Touro, the scourge of anti-Semitism still exists. However, efforts to fight this menace to religious freedom—to educate and to increase awareness—are taking place.

America's Commitment to Fighting Hate

In May 2023 President Joe Biden introduced a US government initiative to address the problem of anti-Semitism. In announcing this initiative, he said, "The past several years, hate has been given too much oxygen, fueling a rapid rise in antisemitism. It's simply wrong. It's not only immoral, it's unacceptable. It's on all of us to stop it."[42] The US National Strategy to Counter Antisemitism has four main goals: to increase awareness and understanding of antisemitism and Jewish American heritage; to improve safety and security for Jewish communities;

to reverse the normalization of antisemitism and counter antisemitic discrimination; and to build cross-community solidarity and collective action to counter hate.

> "[The government] gives to bigotry no sanction, to persecution no assistance."[41]
>
> —George Washington

Such an ambitious plan requires cooperation from segments of society as varied as the high-tech sector, sports leagues, the entertainment industry, and civil rights organizations, among others. For example, in October representatives of many professional sports leagues convened to discuss ways to combat anti-Semitism and other forms of hate. More than one hundred companies and organizations have signed a "Workplace Pledge to Fight Anti-Semitism" provided by the ADL.

Learning About Anti-Semitism

The US National Strategy to Counter Antisemitism is a historic first step in a coordinated federal effort to fight anti-Semitism. But individuals are already becoming educated and taking action on their own to address the problem. In 2021 Sam Zahn, a student at the University of North Carolina at Chapel Hill, realized that the school did not offer any courses dealing with anti-Semitism. Zahn collaborated with Max Lazar, a graduate student at the university, to develop a new course called Topics in Jewish Studies: Confronting Anti-Semitism. The course features weekly guest speakers and covers

A United States postage stamp printed in the 1980s commemorated George Washington's reaffirmation of America's commitment to religious liberty.

topics such as the history of anti-Semitism and methods to counter anti-Semitism both on campus and in the community. Zahn's initial concern that few students would sign up for the course was soon replaced with struggles to find adequate classroom space.

One of the most effective ways to combat anti-Semitism is to teach students at all levels—elementary, high school, and college—about the dangers that anti-Jewish hate poses to society. On the same day that the Biden administration unveiled the US National Strategy to Counter Antisemitism, the US Department of Education created the Antisemitism Awareness Campaign, which intends "to provide all students, including students who are or are perceived to be Jewish, a school environment free from discrimination."[45] The campaign will include visits to schools to ensure cooperation in fighting discrimination, highlight efforts by students and teachers who successfully address anti-Semitism, and assist schools in being more accepting of students of all faiths.

In 2021 students at the University of North Carolina at Chapel Hill developed a course titled Topics in Jewish Studies: Confronting Anti-Semitism. Defying expectations, the course proved to be so popular that the university struggled to find adequate classroom space.

Education about the history of violence against the Jews is important to the understanding of anti-Semitism, especially for young people. In a 2018 study by the nonprofit organization Claims Conference, 22 percent of millennials surveyed said they had never heard of or were uncertain about the Holocaust. In addition, 41 percent believe that 2 million or fewer Jews died in the Holocaust, and almost half could not name even one concentration camp (out of forty thousand).

Many nonprofit organizations provide information on combating anti-Semitism for classroom use. The ADL partners with schools to challenge racial and religious hate, including antibias education, confronting bullying and cyberbullying, and Holocaust and anti-Semitism education. One ADL initiative is BINAH: Building Insights to Navigate Antisemitism & Hate. Developed as digital lessons for high school students, BINAH covers Jewish history, Jewish life today, how anti-Semitism impacts society, and how students can respond to anti-Semitism and support the Jewish community.

The ADL also created Words to Action, an interactive educational program, in response to a survey of Jewish students conducted in New England. Middle and high school students who were surveyed reported personally experiencing anti-Semitism in their schools and neighborhoods but said they rarely knew how to deal with these hateful provocations. Words to Action empowers these students to stand up for themselves and create effective responses to anti-Semitic harassment. The program is conducted in schools, university campuses, summer camps, synagogues, and other venues. Students come away from the program with a better understanding of who they are. "I learned how important it is to stay strong and know the facts," notes a Denver high school student, "so you can stand up for yourself."[46]

Taking Action Against Anti-Semitism

Once people are educated in the reasons and prejudices behind anti-Semitism, the next step is to take action to combat the hate. In May 2021 an outbreak of violence between Israelis

> "Antisemitism is alive and well. All we can do is continue to fight it and combat it."[47]
>
> —Shabbat Angels founder Remi Franklin

and Palestinians brought a rise in anti-Semitism in Jewish communities worldwide. Because of the increased tensions, Jews feared being assaulted as they made their way to synagogue on Friday nights and Saturdays to celebrate Shabbat. That is when a Jewish entrepreneur and martial arts expert saw a need for action.

Remi Franklin was angered by news of an anti-Semitic attack on Jewish patrons at a Los Angeles restaurant in 2021 and vowed to help combat such hate. He recruited a group of volunteers who, like him, had a background in martial arts or were military veterans. Together they formed an organization called Shabbat Angels. The name comes from a story of two angels who accompany each Jew home from their religious services. The volunteers received training centered on de-escalating a threatening incident, defusing an attacker's anger instead of risking the escalation of violence. Once trained, members escort Jews to their synagogue, their presence providing an effective deterrent to anyone who may wish to harass or otherwise harm those in their care. "Antisemitism is alive and well," notes Franklin. "All we can do is continue to fight it and combat it."[47]

The Blue Emoji

Anti-Semitism is an immense international problem, and it often seems to be too overwhelming for the ordinary person even to begin to overcome. But there are numerous small things that can be done to fight anti-Semitism, and one of them involves the global reach of social media.

The Foundation to Combat Antisemitism is a nonprofit organization founded by Robert Kraft, owner of the New England Patriots. The organization has launched a $25 million national campaign called #StandUpToJewishHate to raise awareness about anti-Semitism and encourage both Jews and non-Jews to join the fight against hate. As a symbol of this commitment, people are urged to show Jewish solidarity by adding a blue square emoji to text messages or emails. The blue square can be edited into photos as well.

During the first episode of season 23 of the hit TV show *The Voice*, a blue square emoji was superimposed onto the screen. The emoji took up 2.4 percent of the screen, representing the percentage of Jews in the US population, a group that suffers from 55 percent of all hate crimes committed.

In St. Louis, Missouri, teams of Jewish students visit schools several times a year in a program to help break down Jewish stereotypes and discuss their faith with non-Jewish students. The program is called Student to Student, and it allows the teenage presenters to share their personal experiences and dispel the numerous myths that surround Jews and Judaism. Although a national program, Student to Student operates through local Jewish organizations in St. Louis and dozens of other cities across the nation. During the 2021–2022 school year, teams reached nearly seven thousand high school students, and their visits have had a measurable impact. More than 80 percent of students who attended Student to Student presentations have shared what they learned with others or sought further information. And 27 percent reported that they have disrupted an anti-Semitic remark. "We need to have a conversation with ourselves personally," says Sam Loiterstein, a Student to Student group leader, "and say, 'Am I the kind of bystander that chooses the side of the oppressor?' It's these tiny little acts of courage from the bystanders that make hateful rhetoric have less of an impact."[48]

In an era when White supremacist organizations increasingly hold rallies to spread their rhetoric, other rallies against anti-Semitism are helping raise awareness of the threat that anti-Jewish hatred poses. On January 5, 2020, some ten thousand people, Jews and non-Jews alike, marched in New York City in what was called the No Hate, No Fear solidarity march to protest recent anti-Semitic incidents in the New York–New Jersey area. In one of the most brutal of those attacks, five people were stabbed at a Hanukkah celebration in a rabbi's home by a man wielding a machete. Rally participants marched across the Brooklyn Bridge to a park where speakers that included New York governor Andrew Cuomo, New York City's mayor, and other civic and religious leaders spoke out against anti-Semitic violence.

The Need for Vigilance

As incidents of anti-Semitism continue to increase, it is becoming more important for law enforcement and anti-hate organizations to collect and organize meaningful data that can be used to thwart hate crimes. The ADL has created an interactive online map called H.E.A.T., which stands for "hate, extremism, antisemitism, and terrorism." Using information gathered from media reports, government documents, and other sources, the map displays recent anti-Semitic incidents across the United States and gives a visual representation of the spread of anti-Semitism and other hate crimes. Individuals or groups can use this information to study or analyze trends.

Fighting Online Anti-Semitism, an international nonprofit organization, searches for anti-Semitic content online and works toward ensuring its removal. The Institute for the Study of Contemporary Antisemitism at Indiana University–Bloomington created a data set using artificial intelligence to identify anti-Semitic words in social media posts. This can identify hateful content that may have slipped past a site's moderators and help them eliminate such content.

While these and other efforts to stem hate speech on social media are ongoing, there is still more to be done. Ted Deutch, chief executive officer of the American Jewish Committee, comments,

In January of 2020 some ten thousand people, Jews and non-Jews alike, rallied in New York City in what was called the No Hate, No Fear solidarity march to protest anti-Semitic incidents in the New York–New Jersey area.

Melanie's Story

A Jewish teenager from Connecticut named Melanie Roloff experienced bullying at school because of her faith. A few years later, after getting help, she wrote about her ordeal and how she was able to overcome it.

> My name is Melanie. I was a victim of hate. . . .
>
> Several years ago, I had no hope. I was experiencing vicious anti-Semitism that no child should have to deal with. . . . I was called a poor and dirty Jew if I brought matzah to school on Passover or dreidels to share with my friends on Hanukkah. I was told I belonged in the Holocaust, in the ovens. . . .
>
> The Anti-Defamation League had a workshop for students and their parents at my synagogue in Stamford, Connecticut, to teach families skills for confronting anti-Semitism. I knew I wanted to contact them. I wanted to be involved. . . .
>
> My message to children all over the world is this: Have hope. Be strong, fight for what you believe, and always tell your mom and dad everything. Being bullied is not OK. It is never OK, and you don't need to accept it or stand for it.

Melanie Roloff, "Anti-Semitic Bullies Targeted Me in School. Now I'm Fighting for Other Jewish Children," *USA Today*, October 1, 2018. www.usatoday.com.

"Social media companies must do more in the fight against anti-semitism, first by ensuring their platforms are not used as launching pads for conspiracies and hate targeting Jews."[49]

Reporting Hate Crimes

For many Jews who are victims of anti-Semitic violence or harassment, such assaults can create fear, shame, or a psychological state that makes them reluctant to discuss the incident with others, including law enforcement. In fact, more than eight out of ten Jews who were personally targeted for anti-Semitic violence or harassment did not report the event. Without such feedback, it is difficult for law enforcement and anti-hate organizations to compile statistics on the spread of anti-Semitism, as well as gather information needed to apprehend offenders. While it can be daunting to find the courage to recount an anti-Semitic incident, especially for the victim, there are new ways to report these occurrences that can help in the fight against anti-Semitism.

The ADL works with law enforcement through its twenty-five US regional offices. It provides an online form that can be used to report anti-Semitic incidents for its own statistical purposes, as well as help police agencies track and deter hate crimes. The ADL's Center on Extremism provides law enforcement with intelligence about extremist activities and supports tougher hate crime laws in all fifty states.

Anti-Semitism and Democracy

Fighting anti-Semitism is not only the ethical thing to do, it is a vital factor in the protection of freedom and democracy. Anti-Semitism is an ever-increasing threat to these principles that Americans and others around the world cherish. As expert in Holocaust and genocide studies at Claremont McKenna College in Claremont, California, John K. Roth explains:

> Democracy encourages freedom of speech. Without that freedom, democracy would scarcely exist. But the quality of words matters. When they spew antisemitism and condone anti-Jewish attitudes and actions—sometimes by saying nothing—threats against democracy multiply. Democracy is vulnerable to antidemocratic power. To the extent that antisemitism exists, democracy does not. Whenever antisemitism is curbed and thwarted, democracy's chances get better.[50]

Defeating antisemitism means equality for Jews, a better nation for Americans of every faith, and a stronger democracy that can thrive in a perilous world.

SOURCE NOTES

Introduction: The Oldest Hatred Enters the Twenty-First Century

1. Quoted in Ruth Graham, "Antisemitic Incidents Reach New High in U.S., Anti-Defamation League Says," *New York Times*, March 23, 2023. www.nytimes.com.

Chapter One: The Long History of Anti-Semitism

2. Quoted in Holocaust Memorial Day Trust, "9 November 1938: Kristallnacht." www.hmd.org.uk.
3. Exodus 20:3 (Torah).
4. Matthew 27:25 (New Revised Standard Version).
5. 1 Thessalonians 2:15 (New Revised Standard Version).
6. Quoted in Noam E. Marans, "On Luther and His Lies," *The Christian Century*, October 25, 2017. www.christiancentury.com.
7. Quoted in Yasmin Sabina Khan, *Enlightening the World: The Creation of the Statue of Liberty*. Ithaca, NY: Cornell University Press, 2010, p. 166.
8. Leonard Dinnerstein, *Antisemitism in America*. New York: Oxford University Press, 1994, p. 50.
9. Adolf Hitler, *Mein Kampf*, trans. Ralph Manheim. London: Hutchinson, 1969, p. 294.
10. Quoted in History, "Preparations for the Final Solution Begin," July 29, 2020. www.history.com.
11. Dinnerstein, *Antisemitism in America*, p. 250.
12. Quoted in Sabine von Mering, "The Dark Side of Social Media: How It Fuels Antisemitism," Brandeis University, May 13, 2022. www.brandeis.edu.
13. Quoted in Politico Staff, "Full Text: 2017 Donald Trump Inauguration Speech Transcript," Politico, January 20, 2017. www.politico.com.
14. Quoted in Josh Nathan-Kazis, "Trump's 'America First' Leaves Jewish Groups Hesitant," *Forward*, January 20, 2017. www.forward.com.

Chapter Two: Violence Against Jews

15. Quoted in Tracey Tully and Shlomo Schorr, "F.B.I. Warns of Threat to Synagogues in New Jersey," *New York Times*, November 3, 2022. www.nytimes.com.
16. Quoted in Kevin Roose, "On Gab, an Extremist-Friendly Site, Pittsburgh Shooting Suspect Aired His Hatred in Full," *New York Times*, October 28, 2018. www.nytimes.com.
17. Josh Lipowsky, "Anti-Semitism Resurgent: Manifestations of Anti-Semitism in the 21st Century," Counter Extremism Project, 2023. www.counterextremism.com.

18. Micah Halpern, "Antisemitism and Jew-Hatred Are Not the Same—Opinion," *Jerusalem Post*, November 15, 2022. www.jpost.com.
19. Quoted in Jewish Virtual Library, "Shootings Targeting American Jews (1999–Present)." www.jewishvirtuallibrary.org.
20. Quoted in Investigative Project on Terrorism, "United States District Court, District of New Jersey, Criminal Complaint: *United States of America v. Dion Marsh*, April 19, 2022." www.investigativeproject.org.
21. Joshua M. Davidson, "The Spirit of Emanu-El," Temple Emanu-El, September 29, 2019. www.emanuelnyc.org.

Chapter Three: Anti-Semitic Intimidation

22. Quoted in Andrew Lapin, "'You're on the Path to Sin': A Florida Rabbi Faced Antisemitic Harassment After Speaking Up at a School Board Vote," Jewish Telegraphic Agency, June 15, 2023. www.jta.org.
23. Quoted in Lapin, "'You're on the Path to Sin.'"
24. Stephen Collinson, "A New Wave of Antisemitism Threatens to Rock an Already Unstable World," CNN, October 31, 2023. www.cnn.com.
25. Quoted in Anti-Defamation League, "Hate Symbol: 14 Words." www.adl.org.
26. Quoted in Campaign Against Anti-Semitism, "Police Arrest Man After Van Covered in Antisemitic, Neo-Nazi Slogans Drives Through Florida," May 14, 2021. www.antisemitism.org.
27. Quoted in Jewish Community Relations Bureau and American Jewish Committee, "PREP: Schools and Students: Anti-Semitism in Schools Survey," 2023. www.jcrbajc.org.
28. Jewish Community Relations Bureau and American Jewish Committee, "PREP."
29. Quoted in Danielle McLain, "Campus Leaders React to Growing Antisemitic Vandalism, Harassment," Higher Ed Dive, March 24, 2023. www.highereddive.com.
30. Quoted in Rachel Polansky, "Pandemic Gives Rise to Anti-Semitic 'Zoom Bombing' Attacks in Ohio," WKYC-TV, May 6, 2021. www.wkyc.com.

Chapter Four: Fueling the Fire of Anti-Semitism

31. Quoted in Haley Cohen, "Shabbat Passes Peacefully Despite 'Day of Hate,'" *Jerusalem Post*, February 26, 2023. www.jpost.com.
32. AJC Global Voice, "American Jewish Committee Urges Social Media Firms to Confront Antisemitism on Platforms," February 21, 2023. www.ajc.org.
33. John Earnest, "An Open Letter," Bard Center for the Study of Hate, April 27, 2019. www.bcsh.bard.edu.
34. Quoted in Anti-Defamation League Center on Extremism, "'Ye Is Right' Anti-Semitic Campaign Continues," February 12, 2923. www.adl.org.
35. Quoted in TOI Staff, "Kanye West Says He'll Go to 'Death Con 3 on JEWISH PEOPLE' After Instagram Ban," *Times of Israel*, October 9, 2022. www.timesofisrael.com.

36. Quoted in Emma Green, "Why the Charlottesville Marchers Were Obsessed with Jews," *The Atlantic*, August 15, 2017. www.theatlantic.com.
37. Quoted in David Morgan, "White Supremacist Rallies in Virgina Lead to Violence," CBS News, August 12, 2017. www.cbsnews.com.
38. Quoted in Jack Stripling, "Colleges Braced for Antisemitism and Violence. It's Happening," *Washington Post*, October 31, 2023. www.washingtonpost.com.
39. Quoted in Daniel Arkin, Tom Winter and Dennis Romero, "Cornell University Student Threatened to Stab and Rape Jewish Students and 'Shoot Up' School, Prosecutors Say," NBC News, October 31, 2023. www.nbcnews.com.
40. Catherine E. Lhamon, "Dear Colleague Letter," US Department of Education, Office for Civil Rights, November 7, 2023. https://www2.ed.gov.

Chapter Five: Responding to Anti-Semitism

41. Quoted in National Archives, "From George Washington to the Hebrew Congregation in Newport, Rhode Island, 18 August, 1790." www.founders.archives.gov.
42. Quoted in Nikki Carvajal, "White House Lays Out First-Ever National Strategy to Combat Antisemitism," CNN, May 25, 2023. www.cnn.com.
43. Quoted in AJC Global Voice, "What the U.S. National Strategy to Counter Antisemitism Means for Jewish College Students," August 10, 2023. www.ajc.org.
44. Quoted in Jonathan Guyer, "The High-Stakes Debate over How the US Defines 'Antisemitism,'" Vox, May 25, 2023. www.vox.com.
45. US Department of Education, "U.S. Department of Education Launches Antisemitism Awareness Campaign," May 25, 2023. www.ed.gov.
46. Quoted in Mountain States ADL, "What Our Students Say." www.mountainstates.adl.org.
47. Quoted in AJC Global Voice, "Antisemitism Behind the Numbers: Four Stories About What It's like to Be Jewish in America," October 25, 2021. www.ajc.org.
48. Quoted in Gabrielle Hays, "How Teens in Missouri Are Experiencing Anti-Semitism—and What They're Doing About It," PBS, May 22, 2023. www.pbs.org.
49. Quoted in AJC Global Voice, "American Jewish Committee Urges Social Media Firms to Confront Antisemitism on Platforms."
50. Quoted in Chauncey DeVega, "Trump Leans on George Soros for Campaign Cash," Salon, July 19, 2023. www.salon.com.

ORGANIZATIONS AND WEBSITES

American Jewish Committee (AJC)
www.ajc.org
The AJC is an advocacy organization for the international Jewish community. Working globally with the leadership of government and industry, it promotes the welfare and rights of Jews worldwide. The AJC's website includes resources to help fight anti-Semitism, including the AJC Campus Library with information designed for students.

Anti-Defamation League (ADL)
www.adl.org
The ADL fights anti-Semitism and all forms of bigotry, defends democratic ideals, and protects civil rights for all. Its website offers a resource library with a wealth of articles and other publications about religious, racial, and ethnic discrimination.

My Jewish Learning
www.myjewishlearning.com
My Jewish Learning is a comprehensive website for anyone interested in understanding Jewish history, its faith, and its people. It includes information on Jewish immigration and the Israeli-Palestinian conflict, a Holocaust timeline, and quizzes about various aspects of Jewish life.

Southern Poverty Law Center (SPLC)
www.splcenter.org
The SPLC is a nonprofit legal organization dedicated to fighting all types of civil rights violations, including the activities of White supremacist groups. Its website includes an interactive Hate Map that tracks hate groups in all fifty states. It also publishes numerous articles and publications on various aspects of hate-generated activity.

United States Holocaust Memorial Museum
www.ushmm.org
This museum in Washington, DC, maintains a website with extensive information about the Holocaust. It includes a section on Holocaust denial, which features articles, videos, and notes for discussion about the role of the Holocaust in inciting anti-Semitism.

FOR FURTHER RESEARCH

Books

Diana Fersko, *We Need to Talk About Antisemitism*. New York: Seal, 2023.

Jonathan Greenblatt, *It Could Happen Here*. New York: Mariner, 2022.

Steven L. Jacobs, *Antisemitism: Exploring the Issues*. Santa Barbara, CA: ABC-CLIO, 2020.

Deborah E. Lipstadt, *Antisemitism Here and Now*. New York: Schocken, 2019.

Mark Oppenheimer, *Squirrel Hill: The Tree of Life Shooting*. New York: Knopf, 2021.

Barbara Sheen, *Jewish in America*. San Diego, CA: ReferencePoint, 2021.

Internet Sources

Paul J. Becker and Art Jipson, "Replacement Theory Isn't New—3 Things to Know About How This Once-Fringe Conspiracy Has Become More Mainstream," The Conversation, May 25, 2022. www.theconversation.com.

Simone Carter, "Celebs Besides Kanye Who Faced Backlash over Antisemitic Comments," *Newsweek*, October 26, 2022. www.newsweek.com.

NBC News, "Tracing the Roots of Anti-Semitism with Deborah Lipstadt: Podcast & Transcript," May 15, 2019. www.nbcnews.com.

Jonathan Sarna, "Anti-Semitism in America," My Jewish Learning. www.myjewishlearning.com.

United States Holocaust Memorial Museum. "Origins of Neo-Nazi and White Supremacist Terms and Symbols: A Glossary." www.ushmm.org.

INDEX

Note: Boldface page numbers indicate illustrations.

algorithms, 47
"America first" slogan, 18–19
American Jewish Committee (AJC), 34, 41, 60
Anti-Defamation League (ADL), 7–8, 19, 23, 60
  on anti-Semitic harassment, 29, 32, 42
  efforts to combat anti-Semitism by, 47, 51, 55
  on trend in anti-Semitic incidents, **36**
  on violent anti-Semitic incidents, 20
anti-Semitic incidents
  after October 7 Hamas attack on Israel, 42
  attacks on synagogues, 20–24, 25–26, 37, 38, 42
  hate literature, 39–40
  online harassment, 37–38
  trend in, **36**
  vandalism/desecration, 36–37
anti-Semitism
  on college campuses, 34–35
  important events in history of, **4–5**
  Jew-hatred *vs.*, 24–25
  symbols of, 29–31
  as threat to democracy, 56
  in US history, 6–7, 13
Antisemitism Awareness Campaign (US Department of Education), 50
Arbeit Macht Frei inscription, 32–33, **33**
Auschwitz (death camp), 17, 33, **33**

Babylonians, 11
Biden, Joe/Biden administration, 48, 50
BINAH: Building Insights to Navigate Antisemitism & Hate initiative (ADL), 51
Bowers, Robert, 22–24
Buchenwald (death camp), **17**
Buxbaum, Elissa, 35

Chelmno (death camp), 16
civil rights movement, 21
Cold War, 17
Collinson, Stephen, 29
Confederate battle flag, 31
Coulibaly, Amédy, 26
Counter Extremism Project, 24
Cuomo, Andrew, 53

Dachau (concentration camp), 16
Davidson, Joshua M., 27–28
Dearborn Independent (newspaper), 18
Department of Education, US, 47, 50
Department of Homeland Security, US, 28
Deutch, Ted, 54–55
Dinnerstein, Leonard, 15, 18
"dog whistle" phrases, 37

Earnest, John Timothy, 25–26
echo symbol, 31

Federal Bureau of Investigation (FBI), 20, 21

Fields, James Alex, Jr., 45
First Amendment, 31
Fong, Jonathan, 32
Ford, Henry, 18
Foundation to Combat Antisemitism, 52
Frank, Anne, 35
Frank, Leo, 23
Franklin, Remi, 52

Gilbert-Kaye, Lori, 25, 26
Goldberg, Efrem, 32
Goyim Defense League (GDL), 33, 35, 40, 43
Greenblatt, Jonathan, 42

Halpern, Micah, 24
Hebrew Benevolent Congregation Temple bombing (Atlanta, 1958), 20–21
Heydrich, Reinhard, 16
Hitler, Adolf, 16, 18, 44
Holocaust, 7, 10
   denial of, 35
   survey on millennials' awareness of, 51
   victims of, **17**
Hyper Cacher grocery store shooting (Paris, 2015), 26

Institute for the Study of Contemporary Antisemitism (Indiana University–Bloomington), 54
Israel
   anti-Semitic incidents after October 7 Hamas attack on, 42
   establishment of, 45

Jew-hatred, anti-Semitism *vs.*, 24–25

Jewish Community Relations Bureau, 34
Jews
   Babylonian exile of, 11
   great migration and, 14–15
   insults aimed at, 33–34
   under Roman occupation, 12
   in US population, 24

Kraft, Robert, 52
Kristallnacht ("Night of Broken Glass," 1938), 10, **11**
Ku Klux Klan, 19, 22, 23, 31

Lakewood anti-Semitic crime spree (NJ, 2022), 26–27
Lazar, Max, 49
Lazarus, Emma, 14–15
Lent, Taylor Roslyn, 46
Levin, Brian, 7
Levy, David, 20
Loiterstein, Sam, 53
Luther, Martin, 12–13

Marsh, Dion, 27
Mein Kampf (*My Struggle*, Hitler), 16, 18
mezuzah, 35
Miller, Adam, 29
Miller, Cassie, 18
monotheism, 11
Moore, Deborah Dash, 19
Moses, 11
My Jewish Learning (website), 60

"New Colossus, The" (Lazarus), 14–15
Ninety-Five Theses (Luther), 12
No Hate, No Fear solidarity march (New York City, 2020), 53, **54**

Oath Keepers, 19

On the Jews and Their Lies (Luther), 12–13
opinion polls. *See* surveys
Orthodox Chabad of Poway shooting (CA, 2019), 25–26

Palestine/Palestinians, 9, 51–52
Paul (saint), 12
Phagan, Mary, 23
pogroms, 15
polls. *See* surveys
Protestant Reformation, 12
Protocols of the Elders of Zion, The, 44
Proud Boys, 19

racial anti-Semitism, 13
Roloff, Melanie, 53
Rosenthal, Cecil, 23
Rosenthal, David, 23
Roth, John K., 56
Rothschild, Jacob M., 21

Shabbat Angels, 52
shoelaces, as political statement, 32
Sibony, Zarie, 26
Simon, Bernice, 23
Simon, Sylvan, 23
social media
  combating anti-Semitism on, 52
  in spread of anti-Semitic misinformation, 41–42
Southern Poverty Law Center (SPLC), 18, 60
#StandUpToJewishHate campaign, 52
State of Antisemitism in America 2022, The (American Jewish Committee), 41
Student to Student program, 53
Stuyvesant, Peter, 7
surveys
  on anti-Semitism as serious problem, 42
  on anti-Semitism online, 41
  of millennials, on awareness of the Holocaust, 51
  of youth on experiencing forms of anti-Semitism, 34
swastika, **30**, 30–31
symbols, of anti-Semitism, 29–31
synagogue(s), 15
  attacks on, 20–24, 25–26, 37, 38, 42
  destruction of, on *Kristallnacht*, 10, **11**
  first, in New World, 48
  increasing security at, 20, **27**, 27–28

Touro Synagogue (Newport, RI), 48, **49**
Tree of Life synagogue shooting (Pittsburgh, 2018), 22–24
Trump, Donald, 18–19

United States Holocaust Memorial Museum, 60
Unite the Right rally (Charlottesville, VA, 2017), **8**, 44–45, **45**
US National Strategy to Counter Antisemitism, 48–49, 50

Washington, George, 48
White supremacists/supremacy, **8**, 9, 43, 44–45, **45**, 53
  rise of, 18–19
  symbols used by, 31, 32
Words to Action (educational program), 51

Ye (Kanye West), 43

Zahn, Sam, 49, 50
Zionism, 45
Zoombombing, 38

64